WALCH  PUBLISHING

MW00907754

Daily Warm-Ups

CRITICAL
THINKING

Deborah Eaton

Level I

The classroom teacher may reproduce materials in this book for classroom use only.
The reproduction of any part for an entire school or school system is strictly prohibited.
No part of this publication may be transmitted, stored, or recorded in any form
without written permission from the publisher.

ISBN 0-8251-5059-0
Copyright © 2004
Walch Publishing
P.O. Box 658 • Portland, Maine 04104-0658
walch.com
Printed in the United States of America

Table of Contents

The **Daily Warm-Ups series** is a wonderful way to turn extra classroom minutes into valuable learning time. The 180 quick activities—one for each day of the school year—help students practice critical-thinking skills in language arts, math, social studies, science, and life skills. They may be used at the beginning of class to get students into thinking mode, near the end of class to make good use of transitional time, in the middle of class to help students shift gears between lessons—or whenever you have minutes that now go unused. In addition to helping students warm up and focus, they are a natural lead-in to other classroom activities involving critical-thinking skills. As students build their critical-thinking skills, they will be better prepared to tackle standardized tests as well.

Daily Warm-Ups are easy to use. Simply photocopy the day's activity and distribute it. Or make a transparency of the activity and project it on the board. You may want to use the activities for extra credit points or as a check on your students' critical-thinking skills as they are acquired and built over time. Each activity is rated with one to three stars to identify difficulty level:

    * = basic
   ** = intermediate
  *** = advanced

However you choose to use them, *Daily Warm-Ups* are a convenient and useful supplement to your regular class lessons. Make every minute of your class time count!

Language Arts

Spell-Wells*

There are a number of sayings people use to remember how to spell certain words. Here is one: *Always remember, your principal is your pal*. Here's another: *A porpoise makes an interesting noise*.

Look at the word list below. Choose four words you might have trouble spelling. Write a sentence or rhyme to help you remember the correct spelling.

absence	deceive	patient
accommodate	doubt	psychology
ascend	extraordinary	pyramid
beauty	government	rhubarb
business	necessary	rhythm
courtesy	parallel	scissors

Plurals*

One cat is spelled *c-a-t*. To make that into two cats, you add an *s* to make *c-a-t-s*. Write all the rules you know for making a word into a plural.

Daily Warm-Ups: Critical Thinking I

2

Will the Real Adjectives Please Stand Up?***

The lines below are from the nonsense poem "The Jabberwocky" by Lewis Carroll. Which words in the rhyme are adjectives? Explain how you can tell.

'Twas brillig, and the slithy toves

    Did gyre and gimble in the wabe;

All mimsy were the borogoves,

    And the mome raths outgrabe.

Language Arts

He Said, She Said**

Author I. M. Beauring just completed his latest novel, *He Said, She Said,* which is written completely in dialogue. However, Mr. Beauring feels the book needs some editing. The word *said* is used over and over again, thousands of times. Can you help this author? Write as many words as you can that might be used in place of *said.* A few are listed to get you started.

explained	elaborated	pronounced	whined
_____	_____	_____	_____
_____	_____	_____	_____
_____	_____	_____	_____
_____	_____	_____	_____

4

Language Arts

Dis-ing**

Below are eight words that begin with the letters *dis*. These words can be sorted into two categories to go with the words in the boxes. Sort the words by writing them on the lines. Then explain the difference between the two groups of words.

| dislike | disorganized | dismayed | dismiss |
| dispute | distinct | disprove | disagree |

Group 1		**Group 2**	
disappear	discontinued	disaster	disturbed
_____	_____	_____	_____
_____	_____	_____	_____
_____	_____	_____	_____

Explanation: _____

_____

Now add some *dis* words of your own to the lists. *Hint:* Think about prefixes!

5

© 2004 Walch Publishing

Sort It!*

Sort the words below into two or more categories. Write the name
of the category at the top of each list.

chickens	geese	wolves	cubs	chicks
dogs	goslings	puppies	foals	deer
ducks	horses	foxes	ducklings	fawns
flocks	cows	kits	calves	blackbirds
packs	herds			

Category: _____   Category: _____   Category: _____

6

In the space below, sort the same words again, a different way.

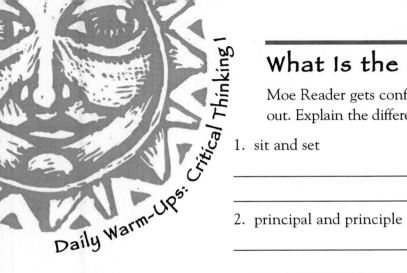

What Is the Difference?**

Moe Reader gets confused about word use sometimes. Help him out. Explain the different meanings of the words in each pair below.

1. sit and set

_____

_____

2. principal and principle

_____

_____

3. accept and except

_____

_____

4. all ready and already

_____

_____

Language Arts

Build Your Own Compounds*

Compound words are two words put together to make a new word. Examples are *snowman*, *basketball*, and *upstairs*. Add to each word below to make as many compound words as you can. Remember, you can add a word to the beginning or to the end!

1. sun _____

2. water _____

3. man _____

4. some _____

5. house _____

6. light _____

7. time _____

8. over _____

8

The Compounds Game**

A compound word is two words put together to make a new word. Sometimes, two or more compound words share the same word part. See how many compounds you can make that share a part. One example has been done for you.

doll and work   <u>dollhouse</u>   and   <u>housework</u>

1. flower and light   _____ and _____

2. tea and table   _____ and _____

3. weed and shell   _____ and _____

4. light and burn   _____ and _____

5. butter and dragon   _____ and _____

6. back and news   _____ and _____

7. light and ache   _____ and _____

8. phone and ring   _____ and _____

9

Synonyms**

No two words mean exactly the same thing. **Synonyms** are words that have similar meanings. The words listed are groups of synonyms. Write them in order by degree, with the least first and the strongest last. One example has been done for you.

run	hustle	<u>hustle</u>	<u>run</u>	<u>race</u>	<u>fly</u>
race	fly				

1. guffaw smile   _____ _____ _____ _____
   laugh   giggle

2. chilly cold   _____ _____ _____ _____
   arctic biting

3. spacious ample   _____ _____ _____ _____
   large   roomy

4. outdo   defeat   _____ _____ _____ _____
   vanquish beat

10

Make a Crossword*

Make a crossword puzzle. Use vocabulary words you have learned. Add numbers in the crossword boxes that match the clues you write.

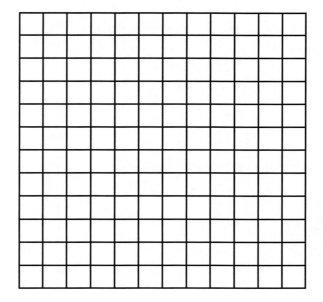

CLUES

Across:

Down:

Do You Speak Greek?***

Many of our English words came from Latin or Greek roots. For example, *spiritus* in Latin means "spirit." From that, we get words like *spiritual*, *spirit*, and *inspire*. Look at the Latin and Greek words below. Write some English words that come from them. One example has been done for you.

12

In Greek, *bi* means "two."

bicycle   biceps   biplane
binoculars   bifocals   biped

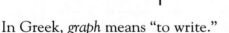

In Greek, *graph* means "to write."

In Greek, *phon* means "sound."

In Latin, *port* means "to carry."

In Latin, *act* means "to do."

In Latin, *unum* or *uni* means "one."

Daily Warm-Ups: Critical Thinking I

Make Your Own Analogies**

Analogies are word pairs that show ways in which words are related to each other. Look at the examples. Then write one analogy of each type.

Synonyms: **work** is to **labor** as **car** is to **automobile**

Antonyms: **hot** is to **cold** as **inside** is to **outside**

Function: **hammer** is to **pound** as **shovel** is to **dig**

Part to whole: **wheel** is to **bicycle** as **roof** is to **building**

Type of: **cardinal** is to **bird** as **trout** is to **fish**

Cause and effect: **joke** is to **laughing** as **cut** is to **bleeding**

Synonyms	Antonyms
Function	Part to Whole
Type of	Cause and Effect

Daily Warm-Ups: Critical Thinking!

13

Language Arts

Goodbye to Clichés!***

A **cliché** [klee-SHAY] is a worn-out way to say something. A **simile** is a comparison using the word *like* or *as*. The similes below are all clichés. Get rid of them for good! Write new similes that are fresh and original. Check out this example:

cliché: He was as cold as ice.

new: He was as cold as a bald polar bear at the North Pole.

1. It was as dark as night.

   _____

2. It happened quick as a wink.

   _____

3. He was as quiet as a mouse.

   _____

4. She is as strong as an ox.

   _____

5. The air is as dry as a bone.

   _____

14

What Am I?***

These riddles were around when your great-great-grandparents were children. The answers are all things you might see every day. Can you figure them out?

1. I go round in circles, but always straight ahead.
    What am I? _____

2. I run all day, but I never get away.
    What am I? _____

3. I have no head, no arms, and no legs.
    But I do have a tongue and a toe.
    What am I? _____

4. I can run, but I cannot walk.
    I have a mouth, but I cannot talk.
    What am I? _____

5. When I am filled, I can point the way.
    When I am empty, nothing moves me.
    I have two skins, one without and one within.
    What am I? _____

Brainstorming 1**

Forget your usual way of doing things. List ten new, original ways to give a book report.

16

Daily Warm-Ups: Critical Thinking!

Language Arts

Brainstorming 2**

Put on your inventor's hat. List ten new, improved ways to use a lemon!

17

How Do You Do It? 1**

You know how to outline a report, right? Imagine that you are teaching a younger student how to make an outline. Below, write your explanation of how to do it.

18

Language Arts

How Do You Do It? 2*

You need to write a report on the moons of Jupiter. Your teacher wants you to use three different sources of information. You decide to look for a book first. When you get to the library, what should you do?

Step 1. _____

Step 2. _____

Step 3. _____

Step 4. _____

Step 5. _____

What are two other sources of information for your report?

1. _____

2. _____

19

Thinking Like an Editor**

You have just finished the first draft of a report for school.
Tomorrow you will revise and edit it. What questions should you
ask yourself as you reread the paper and decide how to improve it?
Use the questions below to get started.

Did I include all the important information?

Can I take out any unnecessary words or sentences?

Do I need diagrams or drawings to help readers understand what I am saying?

20

Is It or Ain't It?*

Why bother to learn good grammar? Is it really important? Write what you think about these questions. List at least two reasons to back up your opinion.

21

The Story of You*

The story of your life has just been published! Write a table of contents for the book.

22

Poetry Challenge***

Two lines that rhyme are called a **couplet.** Finishing the couplets below should be easy. So here is an extra challenge, just to make it interesting. Try to finish each one with a rhyming word whose ending is spelled differently from the word with which it rhymes. Two examples have been done for you.

I tried to learn to <u>ski</u>.   If what he said is <u>true</u>,

Now I have a broken <u>knee</u>!   I'll eat my purple, high-heeled <u>shoe</u>.

1. When Herman tried to fly

    _____

2. The chilly North Wind blows

    _____

3. Be careful what you say

    _____

4. I do not know what to do

    _____

5. Miss Jelly yelled, "Do not go!"

    _____

23

Emily's Thoughts***

Read this poem by Emily Dickinson. A frigate is a ship and coursers are horses. You may use a dictionary to look up other words, if you need to.

> There is no frigate like a book,
> > To take us lands away,
> Nor any coursers like a page
> > Of prancing poetry.
> This traverse may the poorest take
> > Without oppress of toll;
> How frugal is the chariot
> > That bears a human soul!

Now write the message of the poem in your own words.

24

Daily Warm-Ups: Critical Thinking!

Language Arts

What Is He Saying?***

Read this poem by Ralph Waldo Emerson.

> He who has no hands
> Perforce[1] must use his tongue;
> Foxes are so cunning[2]
> Because they are not strong.

[1]by necessity; having no choice
[2]tricky or crafty

1. What does the poem mean?

   _____

2. Can you think of another example besides the fox to prove the poet's point?

   _____ are so _____

   Because they are not _____.

3. What would be a good title for this poem?

   _____

25

What Do You Think?**

Read the following quotations. Tell which one you agree with, and why.

Money is indeed the most important thing in the world.

Money cannot buy happiness.

Daily Warm-Ups: Critical Thinking I

Daily Warm-Ups: Critical Thinking

Language Arts

Proverb 1**

A **proverb** is a saying that might apply to many situations. Read the proverb below. Write what it means in your own words. Then tell whether or not you agree with the proverb, and why.

A stitch in time saves nine.

27

© 2004 © 2004 W

Proverb 2***

A **proverb** is a saying that might apply to many situations. Read the proverb below. Write what it means in your own words. Then tell whether or not you agree with the proverb, and why.

Where there is smoke, there is fire.

28

Language Arts

You for the Defense***

A defense attorney has to present evidence and defend his or her client's character to a jury. Imagine that you are an attorney. Your client is the wolf who huffed and puffed in "The Three Little Pigs." He has been charged with harassing innocent piglets with the intent to harm them. Write a speech to present to the jury. Tell them why they should find your client not guilty.

Note: To harass means "to plague, bother, or worry, especially over a period of time."

29

Language Arts

You're a Poet and You Know It!***

Poems do not have to rhyme. Write a poem. Choose words for your poem ONLY from the words and word bits below.

a	bend	cavort	endeavor
absent	bird	cherish	face
agony	blank	clouds	fascinating
amazed	blind	contrary	faster
an	bumblebees	dolphin	feathered
and	buzzing	earthworm	flicker
are	canine	*-ed*	flight

flush	indifferent	one	splattered	voyage
fox	*-ing*	onyx	stupendous	was
further	is	plod	than	were
gallop	jellybean	prehistoric	that	when
generous	leaves	rise	the	where
gnat	massive	roar	toast	why
gratitude	millions	*-s*	turquoise	wiggles
harmony	musician	sail	under	wish
heart	mysterious	shatter	underbelly	within
hunger	of	sing	useless	write
in	on	snuffling	valuable	wrong

30

© 2004 Walch Publishing

Language Arts

The Best Books***

What book would you like your class to read next? Think about the best books you have read. Then write a paragraph including three reasons that will convince your teacher to choose the book you like best.

31

Language Arts

Fables 1: What's the Moral?**

Every fable has a moral, or lesson to teach. Read the fable below.
Write the moral in your own words.

The Fox and the Crow

A crow and a fox spied a piece of cheese at the same time. The crow
swooped down and snatched the cheese in his beak.

The fox was wily, however. He said, "My, my. I have always admired your
flying abilities, Sir Crow."

The crow fluffed his feathers and nodded vigorously.

"And those feathers of yours. So shiny. So sleek."

The crow nodded again, harder this time.

"Why, if you had a really first-class caw, I think you would be the finest crow in
this forest," the fox declared.

"Mmmph!" said the crow. He still had that cheese in his mouth.

The fox shrugged. "You do not have that mighty voice that the best crows need."

At that, the crow opened his beak and gave a mighty CAW! The cheese
dropped from his wide-open beak.

The fox picked up the cheese. Grinning, he trotted home with his tasty lunch.

The moral is _____

32

Fables 2: One for the Little Kids***

Miss Turry, the second-grade teacher, wants her students to read this fable. It is just a little too hard for them. Rewrite it so that those seven-year-olds can read and understand it.

The Bear in the Wood

Two young companions named Bill and Phil were hiking through a shadowy wood. Suddenly, a ferocious bear leapt out at them. The companions began to flee, as swiftly as they could. Unfortunately, Bill tripped on a tree root and sprawled facedown on the ground. Phil sped on and scampered up a convenient tree. He looked back and spied the gigantic bear approaching his companion. Bill was lying motionless. The bear prodded Bill's shoulder, snuffled for a long time at Bill's ear, then shambled away. At that, Phil scrambled down the tree and came running back.

"Bill! Bill!" Phil said. "That hideous grizzly seemed to whisper right in your ear! Did he? What did he say?"

Bill got up and dusted off his apparel. He answered, "He told me a friend who would leave you in the lurch is no friend at all!"

33

New Kid in School***

Imagine that you have just started school in a country where you do not know the language. The language does not use the same alphabet that English uses. List at least three ways that you can communicate to ask where the cafeteria is.

34

Language Arts

A Quick Story***

Choose one word from each list below. Then quickly write a very short story using those words.

Character
a gym teacher
a bus driver
a principal

Time
late at night
early in the morning
at noon

Place
your school
the grocery store
the woods

Problem
the character sees a crime
the character discovers a secret
the character has a secret
to hide

35

Yawners and Grabbers***

Write two beginnings for the same story. Make the first one dull and ordinary. Write the second one so that you really keep your readers on the edge of their seats.

1. The Yawner

36

2. The Attention-Grabber

Find the Errors*

Josie Fizzbottle was in a hurry when she filled in this multiplication table this morning. How many mistakes can you find? Cross them out and write the correct numbers.

	1	2	3	4	5	6	7
1	0	2	3	4	5	6	7
2	2	4	6	8	10	12	14
3	3	6	9	12	15	20	21
4	4	8	12	16	18	24	35
5	5	10	15	15	25	30	35
6	6	12	15	24	30	36	43
7	7	14	21	27	35	41	49

37

Hiking Around Lake Makatawee**

The counselors from Camp Muskrat are leading a hike tomorrow. They are not sure how many campers will sign up for the trip.

Fill in this trail mix recipe to make enough for about seven people. Then double the recipe, just in case the counselors need more. Your amounts should include some fractions!

Trail Mix Recipe

___ cup(s) peanuts

___ cup(s) almonds

___ cup(s) raisins

___ cup(s) chocolate chips

Doubled Trail Mix Recipe

___ cup(s) peanuts

___ cup(s) almonds

___ cup(s) raisins

___ cup(s) chocolate chips

38

Do Aliens Count?***

An alien is visiting Earth from a planet far, far away. Even the math is different there. The alien would like to learn how to count from 1 to 100. Explain how, in a way that will make it easy for the alien to learn. (*Hint:* Think about patterns!)

39

A Question of Quilting*

Quilters often use triangles in their patterns. Draw a diagram of a quilt square with four triangles for a quilt pattern. Divide one square into halves, the next into fourths, another into eighths. If you want to make your pattern simpler and less busy, should you divide your last square into sixteenths or sixty-fourths? Explain why.

40

How Old Are You?***

Write number sentences that will solve the following problem:

The orbit of the planet Venus around the Sun takes 225 Earth days. The orbit of Uranus takes 84 Earth years. How many years old are you on each planet? Round your answers to the nearest thousandth. (*Hint:* Remember, Earth goes around the Sun every 365 days!)

41

Author, Author!**

Write a short-short story that includes the following number
sentence: 56 divided by 8 equals 7.

42

Math

A Calculated Error*

Sonia Oopsmeyer, who is proud of how fast she can punch numbers into her calculator, divided a number by 40 instead of multiplying it by 40. Her answer, which was wrong, was 20. What is the correct answer? Describe each step you took to find the answer.

Tom's Toolshed***

Tom wants to build a toolshed. He wants the length of the front of his shed to be $\frac{3}{4}$ of the length of the sides of the shed. The length of the sides will be 20 feet. The height of the peak of the roof from the floor will be $\frac{1}{3}$ of the length of the front of the shed. Does Tom have all of the information he needs to build his shed? If you think he does not, write any additional information he needs.

Daily Warm-Ups: Critical Thinking I

44

Will the Real Analogies Please Stand Up?*

Which of the following comparisons are analogies? Explain how you determined which ones are not. *Hint:* An **analogy** means that the relationship of each pair of numbers must be the same.

In these sentences   : means "is to"   and   :: means "as"

1.   4 : 8 :: 32 : 64 (4 is to 8 as 32 is to 64)

2.   103 : 301 :: 4777 : 7744

3.   .75 : $\frac{3}{4}$ :: .40 : $\frac{2}{5}$

4.   17 : 21 :: 1,332 : 1,336

5. $\frac{3}{7}$: $\frac{7}{3}$ :: $\frac{71}{42}$: $\frac{42}{71}$

6.   5 : 55 :: 2 : 23

45

Who Is the Tallest of Them All?**

Jorge is 6 feet 7 inches tall. Elliot is 6.7 feet tall. Nick is 6.07 feet tall. Arrange the three friends in order from shortest to tallest by writing their names where they belong below. Explain how you made your decision.

1. Shortest _____

2. Middle _____

3. Tallest _____

Daily Warm-Ups: Critical Thinking I

46

Knit Picking*

Sam's mother knits and sells hats and scarves. Because scarves are really popular, she sells three scarves and two hats for every five items she knits. Make a chart that shows how many scarves and hats she will sell if she sells forty-five items. Describe any patterns you discover on your chart.

Daily Warm-Ups: Critical Thinking!

Math

A Solid Search*

Your job is to list as many examples of these solid shapes as you can.
Your search may take you all over your home or all over the world!

Cube   **Cylinder**   **Pyramid**   **Sphere**

Daily Warm-Ups: Critical Thinking I

48

© 2004 Walch Publishing

Math

A Liter Jeopardy*

In the game *Jeopardy*, contestants have to think up questions to go with the answers they are given. Invent two questions in the form of word problems that involve the words *liter* and *milliliters*.

Where Have All the Numbers Gone?*

You wake up one morning and discover that all the numbers have disappeared from the world. Make a list of at least ten things that would be different in this new numberless world.

50

Happy Birthday!**

Mr. Foody wants to celebrate his birthday by treating his family to dinner out. He has $35 to spend, and there are four in the family. Write a menu for a restaurant where Mr. Foody can afford to celebrate his birthday.

Math

Right or Wrong?***

Milly was given a choice by her math teacher. She had to choose which was the larger quantity:

450 hundredths × 450 hundredths

or

4.50 × 4.50

Milly chose 450 hundredths × 450 hundredths. She said she made that choice because that equals 202,500 hundredths, which equals 2,025, and 4.50 × 4.50 only equals 20.25.

Was Milly correct? Explain why or why not.

Daily Warm-Ups: Critical Thinking I

52

Math

Teacher for a Day***

Imagine that you are going to help second-graders learn about the concepts of multiplication and division. List some ways you might explain these ideas.

53

Math

Get That Rebound!**

Make a diagram to prove whether the following statement is true or false:

A man drops a ball from the top of a tower that is 100 feet high. Each time the ball bounces, it bounces back up half of the distance it dropped. By the fifth bounce, the ball will bounce up 3.215 feet.

54

The Math Muse**

Write a poem using at least ten math words. You may use rhyme if you wish, but it is not necessary. You may also want to write your poem as a shape poem to bring in geometry!

55

A Business Agreement**

Sunny wants to sell her dirt bike to her classmate Max. Max cannot pay the whole price of the bike at one time, so Sunny needs to write an agreement that states how Max will pay for the bike. Help Sunny by writing the agreement. Be very specific. Sunny wants to be sure she gets paid so that she can give the money to the Red Cross.

56

Pattern Detectors**

The numbers 4, 9, 16, and 25 can be the sums of consecutive odd numbers.

1 + 3 = 4

1 + 3 + 5 = 9

Write the odd number equations for the other two numbers. Do you see any patterns? Describe them.

57

Fingerprints***

In 1994, the FBI received over 34,000 fingerprint cards each day. Describe a method you could use for making a quick estimate of the number of fingerprint cards the FBI received that year. What is your estimate? Now check (you may use a calculator) to determine if your estimate was reasonably accurate.

58

Math

Trouble for Tonio***

Tonio is staying with his parents in a cabin on the shore of Toad Pond. It is a melting hot day. His mother asks him to bring her exactly one quart of water for mixing a batch of lemonade. Tonio has a bucket and two glass jars. He knows that one jar holds five cups and the other three cups, but the jars and bucket have no measurement markings. Can you tell Tonio how to measure that quart of water for the lemonade? Write out your explanation very clearly.

59

Crack the Code***

Antonia's math teacher decided it would be fun to write the morning problem on the board in code. It was not a very interesting code since it only consisted of boxes. Figure out the code by filling in the boxes with the following symbols: + × ( ) −

☐ 4 ☐ 2 ☐ 1 ☐ 3 ☐ 0 = 11

60

Ordering for Four**

Beth is older than Steve is, and she is younger and taller than Keisha is. Steve is shorter and older than Tim is, but Tim is shorter than Keisha is.

Arrange these four in order of age, oldest to youngest, and then by height, tallest to shortest.

61

© 2004 Walch Publishing

Pottery Workshop**

Mr. Clayton's pottery class wants to attend a weekend workshop. The group rate is $500. The individual rate is $200 for the first student and $70 for each additional student.

Explain a way for Mr. Clayton to figure out how big his class must be in order to save money by choosing the group rate.

62

Math

Island Life***

Stanley lives on an island. The groceries are delivered by ferry once every 6 days. The mail comes every 4 days. Every 8 days there is a visit from the mainland library bookmobile. Draw a number line to show how often the mail, groceries, and bookmobile arrive at Stan's island on the same day. Now study your number line. For extra credit, explain another way to arrive at the correct answer without using a number line.

63

Perfect Way to Show a
Perfect Square*

Nicole just could not understand why the number 16 is called a perfect square. She understands concepts better with pictures than with words. Here is how her teacher, Mr. Mathison, decided to explain the idea.

Choose four other numbers, and arrange stars to show that they are perfect squares.

64

Daily Warm-Ups: Critical Thinking!

Rain Gauge**

Your Uncle Ace just bought himself a new rain gauge. He calls you every time it rains to tell you exactly how many inches fell. Make a graph to organize Uncle Ace's reports.

Rainfall:

September 3 — .1 inches
September 4 — 1.02 inches
September 10 — .001 inches
September 12 — .101 inches
September 15 — 2.3 inches
September 22 — .02 inches
September 30 — .22 inches

What was the total rainfall for September?

65

© 2004 Walch Publishing

Your Own Word Problem***

Write a word problem that relates to your day. Make sure you include enough information to solve the problem. Solve your problem on a separate sheet of paper. Then exchange problems with a classmate and solve each other's problem.

66

Bean Counter***

Your dad found a great deal on economy-size jars of beans at the Big Stuff Supermarket. He offers a prize for the person in the family who can make the closest guess to the number of beans in the jar. His only rule is that you cannot dump them out and count them one by one. (He is the only one allowed to do that!) Explain two ways to estimate the number of beans.

67

You Be the Judge***

Do you agree or disagree with Sarah's description of a cube?

A cube is a three-dimensional square solid with five faces, eight vertices, and sixteen edges. Each angle formed is 90 degrees. You find the surface area by adding up the areas of the five faces. For a four-inch cube this would be

Surface Area = 5(4 × 4) = 80 square inches

To find the volume, you multiply the base times the width times the height. This would be

Volume = 4 × 4 × 4 = 64 cubic inches

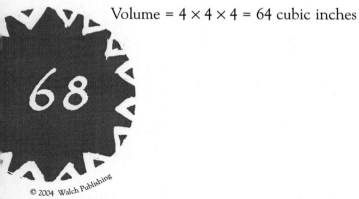

68

Daily Warm-Ups: Critical Thinking!

Forgetful Frank**

Frank has forgotten what the differences are between a sphere and a pyramid. Write a clear explanation for him. You may use examples.

69

Maria Paints Her Room***

Maria wants to paint her room. She has chosen her favorite color, California Orange. Her parents want her to figure out the cost of the paint for the job. Make a list of every measurement and price Maria will need to determine the cost of painting her room.

(*Hint:* Remember, you do not paint glass!)

(*Another hint:* Maria is going to leave the door just as her friend Deb painted it: Hyacinth Purple.)

You may draw diagrams, if you wish.

70

Daily Warm-Ups: Critical Thinking!

Why Did the Chickens Cross the Road?*

Farmer Eggleston's chickens keep wandering across the road to Mrs. Primpo's house. She does not like having chickens in her yard. The farmer wants to prove how much good his flock is doing. He discovers that 4 chickens cross the road to peck at grubs that are destroying the lawn, 5 chickens cross to clean up the birdseed under her feeder, 9 cross to gobble the beetles that are eating her rosebushes, 4 chickens eat grubs and beetles, 6 eat seed and beetles, 3 eat grubs and seed, and 5 eat all three.

Draw a diagram to organize the results. Fill in the blanks for what Farmer Eggleston will tell Mrs. Primpo.

____ of my chickens eat grubs.

____ of my chickens eat birdseed.

____ of my chickens eat beetles.

71

Suddenly a Sub!**

You arrive at school one day to find the principal at the door of your classroom. He tells you that your teacher, Mr. Goodmath, will not be in today and you must be his substitute. You read the lesson plan for math: Explain to the class why the following numbers are the same.

$\frac{1}{4}$, $\frac{25}{100}$, .25, 25%

Write at least two ways that you could do this.

72

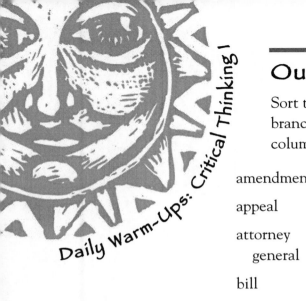

Our Government Word Sort**

Sort the words below to show what you know about the three branches of American government. Write each word in the column where it belongs.

amendment	committee	House	Supreme Court
appeal	Congress	judge	vice president
attorney general	defense	judicial	White House
bill	departments	president	
cabinet	district	prosecutor	
commander in chief	Environmental Protection Agency	representative	
		senator	

73

Executive Branch   **Legislative Branch**   **Judicial Branch**

Tell It to the Alien 1*

An alien has traveled to Earth from a planet far, far away. Everything is very different where the alien lives. The alien has never seen money and does not understand what it is or what it is for. Please explain it to the alien!

74

Social Studies

Tell It to the Alien 2*

An alien has traveled to Earth from a planet far, far away. Everything is very different where the alien lives. The alien has never heard of the word *holiday* and just does not get what it means. Please explain it! Then tell the alien about your favorite holiday.

75

Social Studies

Tell It to the Alien 3**

An alien has traveled to Earth from a planet far, far away. You and the alien are taking a walk when it begins to rain. The alien shrieks and tries to burrow under a rock. Obviously, the alien has never seen rain before. In fact, the alien does not know what water is, either. Please coax the alien out from under that rock. Explain water, rain, and weather.

76

Social Studies

Tell It to the Alien 4**

An alien has traveled to Earth from a planet far, far away. The alien's spaceship happens to land in the United States on election day, November 7, and the alien is very confused by all this activity. The alien has never heard the words *election* or *democracy*. Please explain exactly what people are doing and why.

77

Tell It to the Aliens—Quick!***

A powerful alien spaceship is orbiting Earth. The aliens have sent a message: They do not see the purpose of human beings. They intend to vaporize all humans—unless they hear some very good reasons why they should not. Quick! Write a message to the aliens. Tell them why our lives should be spared.

78

Social Studies

Leadership*

Someday you will vote to decide who should lead your city, your state, and your country. What are some qualities of a good leader? Write the qualities below.

1. _____

2. _____

3. _____

4. _____

5. _____

79

Our USA*

Quick! Write the names of as many of the 50 states as you can.

Daily Warm-Ups: Critical Thinking I

80

Social Studies

City X***

The empty space below is really a blank map. All the land on the map is empty of settlers. When people arrive in the area, where will they build a city, and why will they choose that spot? How will they make their livings, and what will they sell to their neighbors? Put an X on the map to mark the new city. Imagine how it will grow, and write about it. Remember to include a legend that explains the symbols you use on your map.

81

Map It 1**

Draw a map to show the route between your house and the nearest supermarket. Include as many of these map parts as possible: legend, symbols, scale, compass rose.

82

Map It 2**

Draw a map or a house plan showing your idea of the perfect place to live. Be sure to include a key for your map.

83

Would You Buy This Wood?***

Uh-oh. The cost of building a doghouse just got too high. Last month the cost of pine lumber was $1.90 a board foot. This month, the price leaped to $3.10 a board foot. Why? List at least five possible reasons.

84

Social Studies

GCs—Good Citizens*

We all want to be good citizens. But what exactly does that mean? Write your own rules for being a good citizen.

Proclamation

by Me

Hear Ye! Hear Ye! Hear Ye!

From this day forth, all good citizens shall follow the rules below.

85

Rights and What Is Left*

We live in a democracy, and that gives us certain rights. For
example, you have the right to travel and to be protected by laws.
You do not have the right to vote until you are a certain age. List
the rights you have as a young person living in the United States.
Then list some things you do not have the right to do.

I have a right to   I do not have the right to

86

Social Studies

Governmental Perfection***

Design the perfect government. Explain how it would be organized and how it would affect its people.

87

Government, Close to Home**

What kind of government runs things and makes decisions in your home? Is it a democracy? a monarchy? a dictatorship? an anarchy? a plutocracy? Name the form of government in your family, and tell how it works. Give specific examples.

Daily Warm-Ups: Critical Thinking I

88

Social Studies

Be a Tory***

These days, we all take for granted that Americans did the right thing when they fought to free themselves from British rule during the American Revolution. But what if you lived in 1775? Some people, called Tories, thought it was wrong to rebel against the government. Imagine that you are a Tory. List at least five reasons why the American colonies should remain loyal to their British rulers.

89

Tories Again***

At the time of the American Revolution, people who wanted to rebel against the British were called Patriots. They felt that the British government was treating them unfairly and taxing them without giving them enough say in the government. People who felt it was wrong to rebel against Britain were called Tories. They felt any differences could be worked out through the system of government that already existed.

Think about the beliefs of America's President today. Would the President have been a Patriot or a Tory? Back up your decision with at least two good reasons.

90

Daily Warm-Ups: Critical Thinking!

Miss Liberty**

Most people recognize the Statue of Liberty. Why do you think this particular statue is so famous? What does it mean, or symbolize, for the American people? Write one or two paragraphs about it.

91

If You Were There . . .**

Think of an event in history that interests you. Perhaps you are fascinated by the building of the pyramids or by the Wright Brothers' first flight at Kittyhawk. Choose any time and place you like. Imagine that you were there. Write a diary entry about what you might have seen and heard.

Date _____ Place _____

Dear Diary,

92

Social Studies

Advice to Abe***

Think about what you know about President Abraham Lincoln and his life and times. If you could travel back in time, knowing what you know now, what advice would you give to Honest Abe? List at least three pieces of advice.

93

Use Your Magic Wand!***

If you had a magic wand and could change one thing that happened in history, what would it be? How would you change what happened? And how would that make a difference in today's world? Write your changes below.

94

Daily Warm-Ups: Critical Thinking!

Inventions Game 1**

Look at the list of inventions. Of course, you probably do not know the exact year when each one was made. Instead, think about the technology that was needed and have fun trying to put them in order. Write the letter of each one on the time line where you think it belongs. You may be surprised to find out when some inventions were made!

a. bicycle (France)

b. eyeglasses (Italy)

c. lawn mower (England)

d. machine gun (USA)

e. modern printing press (Germany)

f. papermaking (China)

g. parachute (France)

h. pencil (Sweden)

i. steam engine (England)

j. telescope (Italy)

k. windmills (Persia)

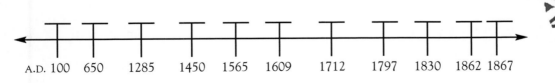

A.D. 100   650   1285   1450   1565   1609   1712   1797   1830   1862 1867

95

Inventions Game 2**

Look at the list of inventions. Of course, you probably do not know the exact year when each one was made. Instead, think about the technology that was needed and have fun trying to put them in order. Write the letter of each one on the time line where you think it belongs. You may be surprised to find out when some inventions were made!

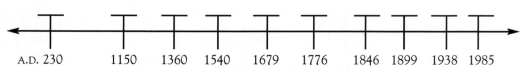

a. artificial limbs (France)

b. aspirin (USA)

c. ballpoint pen (Hungary)

d. compact disc (Japan)

e. gunpowder (China)

f. mechanical clock (France)

g. pressure cooker (Britain)

h. sewing machine (USA)

i. submarine (USA)

j. wheelbarrow (China)

96

A.D. 230   1150   1360   1540   1679   1776   1846 1899 1938 1985

People to People*

In families, in communities, and in countries, the things people do affect those around them. A friend can help a friend. A volunteer can give someone food. A principal can make a new rule. The President can even send people to war. Who affects *your* life? Make a list below.

Person   **How He or She Affects Me**

Social Studies

State Web**

Make a word web about your state. Put the state's name in the
middle circle. Add circles and lines as you add more information.

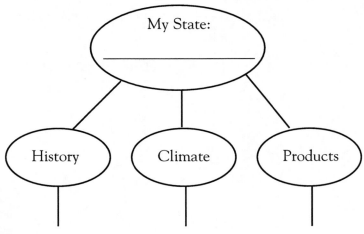

My State:

_____

History   Climate   Products

Daily Warm-Ups: Critical Thinking I

98

Questioning**

Your teacher has asked you to write a three-page report on the slave trade. List ten questions you will want to answer as you do your research.

99

How Do You Do?*

If you could meet any person from history, whom would you like to meet? List some questions you would ask that person.

Name _____

Interview Questions

Daily Warm-Ups: Critical Thinking I

To Go or Not to Go . . .**

Imagine that you live in France in 1730. You have a chance to sail to the New World as an explorer, learning all you can for your country. Would you go? List all the pros and cons below.

Pros: Reasons to Go   **Cons: Reasons Not to Go**

101

Getting to Know Harriet**

You need to write a report on Harriet Tubman, the woman who led many slaves to freedom. Looking for information at the bookstore, you see two interesting books. One is filled with speeches given by Harriet Tubman; the other is filled with personal letters she wrote. You can only buy one of the books. Which one would you buy? Why?

Daily Warm-Ups: Critical Thinking I

102

Social Studies

The Case of the Missing Telephones*

What if the telephone had never been invented? (That means no e-mail or other "instant communication," either!) Uh-oh! No more calling out for a pizza delivery! What else would be different in a world without phones? List at least seven things.

103

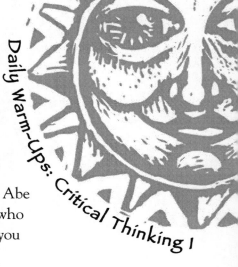

A Name Game **

Did you know that long ago people in a family did not have the same last name? Some boys got their father's first name, plus *son*. That is where last names like Carlson and Stevenson came from. Other people got their last names from where they lived, like John Woods or Mary Rivers. Many people got their last names from what they did for a living. For example, Clive Schumaker made shoes, and Abe Miller ground wheat into flour at his mill. Sam Archer was a soldier who was good with a bow and arrow. How many common last names can you think of that came from people's occupations? Write them below.

104

What Time Is It?***

How well do you know your globe? It is 12 noon, Eastern Standard Time, in New York City. When it is noon in New York, what time is it in each of the cities below? Write each city name beside the correct time.

Panama City   Sydney, Australia   London, England

Los Angeles, California   Mexico City   Bangkok, Thailand

9 A.M. _____

11 A.M. _____

12 noon _____

5 P.M. _____

12 midnight _____

4 A.M. _____
(the next day)

105

Taking a Trip*

Carrie Luggedge has won a trip to exotic Ghana, Africa! She leaves next week. List all the things you think she should learn about Ghana before her plane takes off.

106

Perfect Town***

The people of Perfect Town have passed a law: No dogs are allowed anywhere in town, not even if they are kept inside their own homes. Can the town do that, or is the new law illegal? Why do you think so?

One Hundred Years From Now*

Imagine the world as it might be one hundred years from now.

How will people dress?

How will people travel?

How will people communicate?

How will people earn money?

What will their homes look like?

108

The Black Box Experiment*

Suppose you are given a black box with an unknown object sealed inside. You are told the object is a familiar one, but you may not open the box to see what is inside. Your job is to figure out what the object is.

1. What kind of information can you get about the object from your senses?

   Sight   **Hearing**

   Smell   **Touch**

   Taste

109

2. What kind of tools may help you determine what the object is?

Feather Mystery**

An **adaptation** is a structure or a behavior that makes it easier for a living thing to survive in its environment. Willow ptarmigans are adapted to their environment. They have white feathers at certain times of the year. At other times, they have reddish-brown plumage. What can you guess about willow ptarmigans from this feather mystery? Answer the questions below.

1. Where do you think willow ptarmigans live?

2. When do the birds change color?

3. How do they change color?

4. Why would the color change help the bird survive?

110

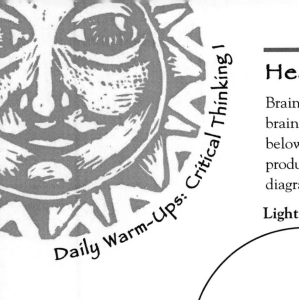

Heat and Light**

Brainstorm a list of all the sources of light you can think of. Now brainstorm a list of all the sources of heat. In the Venn diagram below, categorize the sources that only produce light, that only produce heat, and that produce both light and heat. What does your diagram tell you about the relationship of heat and light energy?

Light Sources   **Heat Sources**

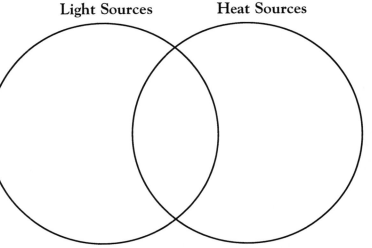

Light and Heat Sources

111

Science

Is There Water on Mars?***

Scientists have sent robots to Mars to search for signs that there has been water on that planet. How do they know what clues to look for? It helps to know what water can do on Earth. Make a list of ways water changes the shape of things on Earth.

112

Nature and You*

Think about how you interact with and are affected by nature. List at least three ways nature affects you in your daily life.

113

Dr. Bunsen's Incredible Discovery**

Dr. Bunsen ran into Professor Quantum's laboratory.

"I have done it! I have done it!" he shouted.

"What have you done?" Professor Quantum asked.

"At last! I have discovered a substance that can dissolve everything it touches."

Professor Quantum looked skeptical. "Really?"

"Yes!" Dr. Bunsen exclaimed. "I have tested it on everything I can think of. It works every time. Shall I bring it to your lab to show you?"

"I do not think you have tested it on everything yet," Professor Quantum suggested.

Why is Professor Quantum so skeptical?

Why is it important for a scientist to be skeptical?

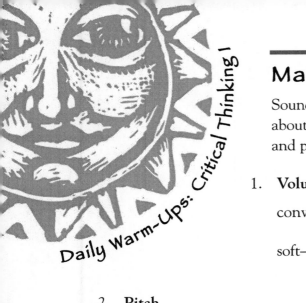

Making Noise*

Sound is a form of energy, made when something vibrates. Think about different groups of sounds and how they differ in volume and pitch. Organize these sounds on the scales below.

1. **Volume**

   conversation   whisper   rock hammer drill   busy playground

   soft————————————————————————————loud

2. **Pitch**

   piccolo   scream   tuba   roll of thunder   laugh

   low————————————————————————high

115

Making Music**

Take what you know about sound waves, pitch, and volume, and design a musical instrument out of everyday materials. Be sure that you can control the pitch and volume of your instrument. Label the materials you would use to make your instrument as well as the part or parts that vibrate.

Daily Warm-Ups: Critical Thinking I

116

The Web of Life**

Organisms must find resources to live, grow, and reproduce. Some organisms are producers, able to produce their own food. Others are consumers and must eat other organisms. Still others are decomposers that consume dead organisms.

Brainstorm a list of organisms that can be found around your home. Categorize them as producers, consumers, and decomposers.

Producers   **Consumers**   **Decomposers**

117

Our Changing Earth*

Earth is always changing. Some changes happen quickly. Others take place over thousands and thousands of years. Brainstorm a list of earth processes. Organize your ideas in two columns: slow changes and fast changes.

Slow Changes

Fast Changes

118

Blizzard Mystery**

Dr. Bunsen lives twenty miles away from Professor Quantum. When it storms, he often gets two or three feet of snow and has to spend hours digging himself out. Professor Quantum only gets two or three inches from the same storm. Can you think of one or more reasons for this weather mystery?

119

Applying Science***

You probably take a variety of classes, including some of the following: language arts, math, social studies, physical education, art, music, foreign language. Choose three classes you take, and tell how science has affected each area of study.

120

Science

Simple Tools for Fun*

A playground has equipment made up of simple machines: the lever and fulcrum, an inclined plane, a screw, a pulley, and a wheel and axle. Think of playgrounds you have visited. Draw a picture or diagram of a playground, and label the simple machines you can find there.

121

Egg Magic*

"Rats!" Dr. Bunsen groaned. He was holding a carton full of eggs in front of him.

"What is the matter?" Professor Quantum asked.

"I cooked a few hard-boiled eggs, but forgot to mark them. Now they are all mixed up with fresh eggs. I guess I will have to crack every one to find the hard-boiled eggs. What a waste!"

"I can sort them for you," Professor Quantum said. She took each one, gave it a spin, touched it lightly, then put it in one of two piles. When she had finished, she pointed to one pile. "These are the hard-boiled eggs."

"Thank you," said Dr. Bunsen. "Would you like to join me for lunch?"

122

How could spinning an egg help Professor Quantum determine which eggs were hard-boiled and which were still uncooked?

Science

The Systems That Are Us*

Human beings are made up of many systems, such as the digestive, excretory, circulatory, respiratory, skeletal, muscular, reproductive, and nervous systems. We can study each of these systems separately, but they really work together to keep our bodies functioning.

Choose two systems, and explain how they interact to make our bodies work well.

123

Gardeners at Work***

Artie Choke and Pete Moss live next door to each other. Both have huge gardens in their backyards. They each spend the same amount of time in their gardens, but Artie's garden is beautiful and extremely productive, while Pete's garden is not doing as well.

What are some of the reasons Pete's garden might not be producing as well as Artie's?

124

Eggcellent Graphing*

Zoë, who lives just outside Madison, Wisconsin, has a flock of ten chickens. She kept track of the eggs her hens laid last year. Here are the numbers.

January: 61	July: 272
February: 147	August: 229
March: 201	September: 208
April: 235	October: 199
May: 265	November: 134
June: 268	December: 68

Make a graph that displays this information. Using the graph, analyze the data. Try to determine possible reasons for the different numbers of eggs laid each month.

125

Science

Life in the Deep, Dark Ocean***

Recently scientists discovered communities of organisms living at hydrothermal vents on the ocean floor. No sunlight ever reaches so far underwater, and the pressure on every square inch of the deep seafloor can be more than 3,000 pounds. Besides that, the vents spew highly toxic, acidic, and very hot (750° F) water into the cold (35° F) water of the deep sea. Quite a different world from the one we know on the surface of Earth!

What questions might scientists ask about these deep-sea vent communities?

126

© 2004 Walch Publishing

Science

Really the Best?***

An advertisement for Sootheeze Cough Drops states: "Best cough drop in the world!"

Hacknomore Cough Drops claim they are "Better than all the rest!"

EZBreathe Cough Drops advertise they are "Unsurpassed!"

Define the qualities you think the best cough drop would have. Then design an experiment that would test the claims of these rival cough drop manufacturers. Be sure you state how you would make your observations, take your measurements, and control variables.

127

The Beginning of Cheese**

There is a story that cheese was first invented long, long ago, when a traveler, wanting something to drink along the way on a hot day, put milk in a container made of a young goat's stomach, then set off on his journey. When he stopped for a drink, he was surprised. The milk had changed into a thin yellowish liquid (whey) full of solid lumps (curds.) The thirsty traveler drank the liquid even though it was not milk, and then tasted the curds. They were delicious! A new food was discovered.

Nowadays, we no longer make cheese by putting milk in a bag made of a goat's stomach. We do make a lot of different kinds of cheese.

From this story, what is necessary to make cheese? What do you think are the variables that make different kinds of cheese?

128

Science

To Your Health**

What are the best ways to keep healthy? Brainstorm a list of important things you can do (and things you should not do) to keep your body strong and safe. Then design a perfect day that includes a balance of activities (including eating meals) that would keep you healthy.

129

Just Like Jack's Beanstalk***

Your family keeps an aloe plant in your kitchen. It has never flowered before, but one year it sends up a flower stalk, which grows amazingly fast. One day it is 8 inches. The next day it is 11 inches, then on following days you measure 15 inches, 18 inches, 21 inches, $23\frac{1}{2}$ inches—and it has not even blossomed yet! You wonder how the stalk grows so fast.

How can you determine how the stalk grows? Does the growth come out of the base of the plant or near the top where all the buds are? Or does every part of it grow at the same speed?

130

© 2004 Walch Publishing

Science

Learning or Instinct?*

Here is a list of human behaviors. Sort them according to whether you think they are instinctual (inborn) or learned. Circle instinctual behaviors. Draw a line under learned behaviors. Then explain how you determine if a behavior is instinctual or learned.

smiling	crying	cooking spaghetti	playing the guitar
writing poems	running	feeling angry	speaking
brushing teeth	eating	pole-vaulting	counting
riding a bike	singing	blinking	speaking Swahili

131

Resources**

Natural resources can be categorized as renewable, nonrenewable, and inexhaustible. List at least three natural resources in each category, and defend your examples.

Renewable   **Nonrenewable**   **Inexhaustible**

132

Daily Warm-Ups: Critical Thinking!

Riding the Continents***

In 1912, Alfred Wegener first proposed a theory stating that the continents, once a single landmass, broke apart and drifted away from one another. How could this theory be proved or disproved? (Consider data gathered in many areas of scientific inquiry, such as geology, oceanography, paleontology, zoology, and geography.)

133

Science

Heat on the Move***

Heat moves from one place to another in three different ways.

- **Conduction** is the movement of energy through a material or between two things that are touching. The energy moves from particle to particle, but the particles themselves do not move. (Think of a spoon in a pot of soup.)

- **Convection** is the transfer of energy by movement of the warm material. This happens most often in liquids or air, when heat moves in currents. (Think of hot air coming from an open oven.)

- **Radiation** happens when electromagnetic waves, such as light, carry energy directly through space. (Think of sunlight warming Earth.)

Draw a picture of one scene that shows all three types of energy transfer. Be sure to label each one.

134

Science

You're the Inventor***

It is your turn to invent something! Think of a problem that could be solved with a new product. Draw a picture of your invention. Explain how it works and why it could take care of the problem. Then look at your invention critically. Evaluate your design based on effectiveness, cost, and unintended consequences.

135

Is It Too Hot in Here?**

Many scientists believe the increase in the amount of carbon dioxide in the atmosphere (caused by industrial activity) is causing Earth's atmosphere to warm up more rapidly than it has for thousands of years. Other scientists see no evidence that Earth's climate is changing for anything other than natural reasons. How would you evaluate competing claims?

Daily Warm-Ups: Critical Thinking I

136

Bugs~B~Gone*

"These bugs are driving me crazy!" Nat said, waving his hands around frantically, trying to get rid of the mosquitoes, flies, bees, and hornets swarming around his head. "I wish insects would all go away!"

Most of us have wished this at one time or another, but what could happen to the ecosystem if Nat got his wish? Give specific examples.

137

When Science Does Not Work*

List five questions that science does not help you answer.

138

Dr. Skeptic's Million-Dollar Prize***

Some people think it is possible to find water underground using a special kind of stick, called a dowsing rod. Dr. Skeptic does not believe it. He offered a million-dollar prize to anyone who could prove dowsing works. To win the prize, the person had to find water in a special field Dr. Skeptic prepared.

The field had three pipes buried underground. There was no way to see where the pipes were. For each test, Dr. Skeptic could let water go into any of the pipes (or all or none of them). The dowser's job was to show where the water flowed through the pipes.

Aqua Phind had three chances to find which pipes held the water by using her dowsing rods. She failed each time. "I have sixty letters here from people who swear I found water for them by dowsing. I claim your million-dollar prize!"

Explain why you think Dr. Skeptic should or should not give Aqua Phind the million-dollar prize.

Daily Warm-Ups: Critical Thinking!

139

How Do They Share?*

Bats, swallows, and dragonflies all eat mosquitoes. They all fly. They all live in the same area. Different species of animals cannot occupy exactly the same niche in an environment. How might these three compete?

Daily Warm-Ups: Critical Thinking I

140

Kitchen Chemistry*

Here are two recipes for cookies:

NO-BAKE TREATS

1 cup honey

$\frac{1}{4}$ cup unsweetened cocoa powder

$\frac{3}{4}$ cup powdered milk

$\frac{1}{2}$ teaspoon salt

2 teaspoons vanilla

$\frac{1}{2}$ cup peanut butter

$\frac{1}{2}$ cup nuts or

    raisins or both

Mix well. Shape into cookies. Eat.

BAKED COOKIES

$\frac{1}{2}$ cup butter

$\frac{1}{2}$ cup honey

1 egg

2 teaspoons vanilla

1 cup whole wheat flour

$\frac{1}{2}$ cup oatmeal

$\frac{1}{2}$ teaspoon baking soda

$\frac{1}{2}$ teaspoon salt

1 cup raisins

Mix butter and honey. Add egg and vanilla. Mix well. Stir in flour, oatmeal, baking soda, and salt. Add raisins. Bake at 350° for 10 minutes.

In one recipe, the matter in it undergoes a physical change. In the other recipe, the matter in it undergoes a chemical change. Which is which? How would you describe physical and chemical changes?

141

© 2004 Walch Publishing

A Cool Scavenger Hunt**

List items in your refrigerator that you can use as examples to explain the following words:

1. mixture _____

   _____

2. solution _____

   _____

3. solid _____

   _____

4. liquid _____

   _____

5. gas _____

   _____

142

Science

We Are So Grateful . . .*

Write a tribute to your muscles, blood, bones, teeth, or other specific parts or systems of your body. Be sure to explain why they are so special to you.

Science

Ode to Weather**

Write a poem using at least ten weather words.

144

Daily Warm-Ups: Critical Thinking!

Be a Television Star**

Nate Treehugger has been chosen to appear on the children's version of a television survival show. He can bring a small backpack full of whatever items he wants. List the items you think Nate should include in his pack and the possible uses for each of them.

145

Life Skills

The Ride Home*

Your uncle is very late! He is supposed to pick you up at school. All the school buses have already left, and you are waiting near the front door. A person you do not know drives up in your uncle's car and says your uncle sent him. He is dressed in a suit and looks perfectly friendly and respectable. What should you do?

146

Home Alone*

Your parents are trying to decide if you will be safe staying home alone while they go out for dinner and a movie. Write the rules you would follow when staying home alone.

147

Dear Know-It-All 1***

Imagine that you write an advice column for young people. How would you answer this letter?

Dear Know-It-All,

My grandmother lives alone, and she says she NEVER wants to move to a nursing home. The other day, when I was visiting her, I noticed she kept forgetting things. She told me the same story three times. And she turned on the cold water faucet when she wanted hot water. I love my grandma, and I do not want her to go away. What should I do? Should I tell?

Regards,
Ann

148

Life Skills

Dear Know-It-All 2***

Imagine that you write an advice column for young people. How would you answer this letter?

Dear Know-It-All,

I have two best friends, Warren Peace and Isabelle Ringing. Yesterday, Isabelle told me that Warren called me a bad name. Warren swears he did not do it. They are both supposed to come to my house for a party this weekend. What should I do?

Help!

Friend in the Middle

149

Dear Know-It-All 3***

Imagine that you write an advice column for young people. How would you answer this letter?

Dear Know-It-All,

My parents are always embarrassing me! They get too excited at my soccer games and yell and whistle until I just want to dig a hole in the field and hide. And they come to school and complain to my teacher over the smallest things. Yesterday they complained because they thought I should have won the class science prize. My entry was not that great. I need advice—quick!

Desperately,

Morty Fide

150

Daily Warm-Ups: Critical Thinking I

Life Skills

Homework*

To do their best work, people have to be comfortable and focused. Rate yourself on how you do homework. Take notes below on each question.

How good is the light where you work?	Do you work in a comfortable upright chair, in a space where you have room to spread out?
Do you have a place to work where there are no distractions? Do you play music or watch television as you complete your homework?	Do you have the supplies you need? pencils? eraser? dictionary? ruler?

How do you think you rate on work space and work habits while doing your homework? What is one way you could improve?

151

Orienteering at the Mall*

There is a big blow-out sale at the mall. You and your mom get there early and park right in the middle of the parking lot. The lot is huge, with thousands of cars. Make three different plans that show how to find your car when you emerge from the mall, laden with packages, three hours from now.

152

Life Skills

Flat!**

Yikes! Ike has a flat tire on his bike, three miles from home. He is in a nice neighborhood, but he does not know anyone around there. What should he do? (*Hint:* He does not have a cell phone.)

153

No, Thanks!**

Some of your friends have taken up smoking recently. They think it is really cool, and they want you to try it, too. What will you say? Write five ways to say no and still keep your friends.

154

Life Skills

Superhero Powers*

You have a choice between two superhero powers. You can become invisible at will OR you can have the power to fly. Which power would you choose?

Give at least two reasons why you chose as you did. Include examples of how you would use your new power.

155

Snackers**

You missed lunch today, and you are so hungry! Dinner is still three hours away. Each snack in the vending machine costs one dollar, and that is exactly what you have in your pocket. Which snack should you choose, and why? Choose from the snacks below.

cheese and crackers   candy bar
tortilla chips   hard candy
apple   cookies

156

Daily Warm-Ups: Critical Thinking!

George's Etiquette**

In 1744, when he was sixteen years old, George Washington wrote a book of manners. Here are some examples of his advice:

- In the presence of others, sing not to yourself with a humming noise, nor drum with your fingers or feet.

- If you cough, sneeze, sigh, or yawn, do it not loud, but privately and speak not in your yawning, but put your handkerchief or hand before your face and turn aside.

- Kill no vermin as fleas, lice, ticks, etc. in the sight of others.

- When you meet one of Greater Quality than yourself, stop and retire, especially if it be at a door or any straight place, to give room for him to pass.

- Gaze not on the marks or blemishes of others or ask not how they came.

Do you think good manners have changed a lot since Washington's day? Tell why or why not.

157

Life Skills

Money: How Much Is It Worth to You?*

If someone offered you $10 to eat a big, fat, juicy earthworm, straight from the mud in a backyard, would you do it? Write yes or no. _____

Would you do it for

$20? _____ $1,000? _____

$100? _____   a million dollars? _____

Tell why you would do it for the amount you chose. (Or why you would not do it at all.)

Daily Warm-Ups: Critical Thinking I

158

Get That Bike!**

You want to buy a new bicycle, but it costs $60 more than you have. Make a plan. Include at least two realistic ways to get the money you need.

My Plan

How much I need:	$60
First source of income:	$60 – _____ = _____ to go
Second source of income:	_____ – _____ = _____ to go
Third source of income:	_____ – _____ = _____ to go
Fourth source of income:	_____ – _____ = _____ to go

© 2004 Walch Publishing

Budget Builder**

Lucky you! Your parents have decided to raise your allowance to $25 per week. But first they want to see your budget. Write one for them.

160

Life Skills

Druthers 1**

Which would you rather do?

- Go to school in a clown suit (and you cannot tell why).
- Be stuck in an elevator with your baby sister for nine hours.

Give reasons for your answer.

161

Druthers 2**

Which would you rather have happen?

- Your dad dances on a table in the school cafeteria.

- Your jeans fall down to your knees as you stand in the lunch line.

Give reasons for your answer.

162

Life Skills

Druthers 3***

Where would you rather wake up?

- in a city park, in a country where you do not speak the language

- in a sailboat in a storm, all alone on a large lake

(*Hint:* Whichever one you choose, you do not have a cell phone!)

Give reasons for your answer.

163

Life Skills

Druthers 4***

If you could travel in time, which would you rather do?

- join a hunting party of Lakota Indians in the Midwest in 1750

- join a battle of the Civil War in 1863

Give reasons for your answer.

Daily Warm-Ups: Critical Thinking I

164

Daily Warm-Ups: Critical Thinking!

School Versus The Real World*

Name at least five ways you might use each of these school subjects in the real world during your lifetime. (You should be able to think of a lot more than five!)

Math   **Language Arts**   **Science**

165

It Is Greek to You**

You just won an all-expenses-paid trip to Greece! Unfortunately, you do not speak Greek, and you have to leave in just a few days. What ten helpful words or phrases would you want to learn to say in Greek?

166

Life Skills

To Tell or Not to Tell***

Your best friend Al has started to drink! You have seen him taking tiny sips out of his parents' liquor bottles. Al thinks it is funny. When you talk with him about it, he just tells you to lighten up. He says he is just fooling around. Should you tell? Why or why not? If you tell, what do you think will happen? What do you think will happen if you do not tell?

167

Cheat, Cheat, Never Beat**

Oh, no! You have been accused of cheating on a math test!

If you did not do it, how could you prove you are innocent?

If you did do it, what should you do now?

168

Life Skills

Which One?*

Swimming lessons and band practice are scheduled at the same time this year. That is too bad, because you wanted to do both. Your friend Mel Odie says playing a musical instrument is lots of fun. Will Float, the swimming instructor, keeps pointing out what good exercise swimming is. Which activity will you sign up for? Give reasons for your choice.

169

© 2004 Walch Publishing

Life Skills

Shedding Pounds*

Roland Butter tends to overeat a bit. He would like to lose 15 pounds. Can you help Roland? Make a plan for him.

Daily Warm-Ups: Critical Thinking I

170

© 2004 Walch Publishing

Where in the World?***

Myles Walker and his sister Lil are going on a trip. Look at the partial packing list below. Where do you think they are going, and what are they going to do there? Why do you think so?

sunscreen

cleats

gloves

water bottles

portable oxygen tank

lip gloss

rope

sunglasses

171

© 2004 Walch Publishing

Tombstones***

Grave markers usually have a person's name and dates of birth and death carved on them. Tombstones in old graveyards often have poems or sayings or other information on them as well.

Think about what you would like your life to be like—how you would like to live and what you would like to accomplish. Then create a tombstone for yourself. Besides your name and the dates you lived, include other information about your life or your beliefs.

172

Life Skills

Fire!**

Your pan of scrambled eggs on the stove has burst into flames! You turn to grab the fire extinguisher in the corner. But then you think you should call 911 instead. Which should you do? Why?

173

Using Information Sources**

Mrs. Spinner wants a spinning wheel for her birthday. Mr. Spinner says he will pay for it, but it is up to his daughter Candy to find one for sale. Candy begins by looking in the Yellow Pages of the telephone book.

What headings should Candy look under to find a spinning wheel?

If she does not find a spinning wheel in the Yellow Pages, where else can she try?

174

Habits*

List all the healthy habits (such as eating vegetables) and unhealthy habits (such as smoking) that you can think of.

Healthy Habits   **Unhealthy Habits**

175

Helping Poor Barkley*

Your family wants to go on a vacation, but your dog, Barkley, cannot be left alone. Barkley cannot stay in a kennel, because of stress. Name five ways you might solve this problem.

176

Perfection***

Design a perfect family. Tell what the family members are like and how they interact. Do you think there would be any drawbacks to living in the perfect family? If so, what are they?

177

Friends to the End*

How good a friend are you? What are you like as a . . .

listener?

supporter?

helper?

sharer?

Write a few sentences rating yourself as a friend.

178

Can You Solve It?***

How good a problem-solver are you? Brainstorm at least ten ways to solve the problem below. Twenty would be even better. (They do not all have to be realistic!)

How could you get a skunk out of an empty swimming pool?

Daily Warm-Ups: Critical Thinking!

179

Can You Sell This Idea?***

Mei really, really, really wants to go to Disney World this year. Her parents are not so sure. List at least ten things she could say to convince them to go.

180

Language Arts

1. Answers will vary.
2. For words ending in *ch, tch, s, x,* and sometimes *o,* add *es* (watches, foxes, heroes). For words ending in *y,* change the *y* to *ie* (pennies). For some words ending in *lf* or *ife,* change to *ves* (calves, knives). There are also irregulars. (For example, change *child* to *children, woman* to *women, tooth* to *teeth, foot* to *feet.*)
3. Accept reasonable answers. Students should call on their prior knowledge of English syntax to understand that sentences are usually organized with subject, verb, and object in order and that adjectives usually precede nouns. The adjectives in the rhyme are *slithy, all, mimsy,* and *mome.* The word *brillig* might also be interpreted as an adjective; however, in his notes, Carroll explained that *brillig* stands for "afternoon."
4. Answers will vary. Examples: answered, replied, argued, remarked, stated, declared, uttered, whispered, shouted, drawled, insisted, informed, stuttered, squawked, announced, bellowed, grunted, related, divulged, purred, growled, sighed
5. In half of the words, *dis* is used as a prefix meaning "not." Those words are *disappear, discontinued, dislike, disagree, disprove,* and *disorganized.* In the other words, *dis* is not a prefix. They are *dismiss, disturbed, dispute, distinct, dismayed,* and *disaster.*
6. Words could be sorted (a) with the three categories of animals that live in flocks, herds, or packs; (b) with the three categories of adult animals, baby animals, and animal group names; or (c) with the three categories of birds, mammals, and animal group names. Also accept any other reasonable answers.
7. 1. You sit with your body, but you set something else in place. 2. A principal is a head of a school, while a principle is a law or a basic truth. 3. When you accept something, you take or receive it; to except means to exclude, or accept everything but.

Daily Warm-Ups: Critical Thinking 1

4. All ready means completely prepared, such as the class is all ready to leave, while already means before now, such as Jack has already left.

8. Answers will vary. Possible answers include
1. sunlight, sunset, sunflower, sunburn, sunglasses
2. seawater, watercolor, waterfall, waterfront, watermelon, watermark 3. snowman, fireman, manhole, workman, fisherman, gentleman
4. somewhere, sometime, someone, bothersome, someday, somebody, something, somewhere
5. housework, housekeeper, dollhouse, doghouse, greenhouse, houseboat, lighthouse 6. sunlight, lighthouse, moonlight, flashlight, headlight, candlelight 7. timetable, sometime, bedtime, suppertime, timepiece, anytime 8. overtime, overpass, overdue, overcast, pushover, overcoat

9. 1. sunflower, sunlight 2. teaspoon, tablespoon
3. seaweed, seashell 4. sunlight, sunburn
5. butterfly, dragonfly 6. paperback, newspaper
7. headlight, headache 8. earphone, earring

10. 1. smile, giggle, laugh, guffaw 2. chilly, cold, biting, arctic 3. ample, roomy, large, spacious
4. outdo, beat, defeat, vanquish

11. Answers will vary.

12. Answers will vary. Possible answers include graph: autograph, graphic, graphite, telegraph; phon: phonics, phonograph, microphone, telephone, symphony; port: portable, transport, import, porter, portage; act: act, actor, action, react, transact, enact; uni: unite, universe, universal, unify, uniform.

13. Students' analogies will vary but should match each category.

14. Answers will vary.

15. 1. a wheel 2. a clock 3. a shoe 4. a river
5. a glove

16. Answers will vary. Give extra points for originality!

17. Answers will vary. Give extra points for originality!

18. Answers will vary. Explanations should include instructions for organizing information in categories and hierarchies of meaning. Students should

explain their system of numbering and lettering entries.

19. Steps should include entering key words into a library search engine or using the card catalog, identifying call numbers, taking notes, finding the correct section of the library, then matching the call number on the book. Other sources of information include encyclopedias, periodicals, and the Internet.

20. Answers will vary but may include the following: Is everything in a logical order? Are paragraphs organized well, with topic sentences? Have I used correct grammar, spelling, and punctuation? Should I vary my sentences more? Have I backed up my statements with examples? Have I used my own words? Does it need quotations to be more interesting or accurate? Is the ending effective—does it summarize my thoughts? Have I used forceful words, especially for adjectives and verbs?

21. Accept all reasonable answers. It might be fun to hold a discussion to help students connect to the possible effects of their use of grammar in the "real world."

22. Answers will vary but should be organized in the form of a table of contents.

23. Answers will vary. Here are some examples of rhyming words with different spellings: 1. sigh, tie 2. rose, froze 3. weigh, Mae 4. new, blue, too 5. low, toe.

24. Accept reasonable answers. The poem is expressing the idea that even if poor, we can take wondrous imaginary trips when we read books.

25. 1. Living things must use whatever strengths and talents they have to survive. 2. Examples will vary. (Bats have sonar because they cannot see well, turtles have shells because they cannot run away, lions have teeth because they cannot purchase their food at the supermarket, and so on.) 3. Titles will vary but should relate to the poem's meaning.

26. Answers will vary. Students should back up their statements with reasons or examples.

27. The saying means that if you do something right

away, as soon as it needs doing, you will probably save yourself time and effort in the long run. Examples are sewing up a rip while it is still small, picking up after yourself before the room becomes very messy, and changing the oil in a car to prevent bigger mechanical problems.

28. The saying means that where there is evidence or clues, you can assume they point to the truth. This may or may not be true. Appearances can be deceiving unless we know all the facts. Accept any reasonable answers.

29. Answers will vary but should include references to the wolf's character, actions, and intentions.

30. Poems will vary.

31. Paragraphs will vary but should be well organized and present cogent arguments, using persuasive language appropriate to the audience of a teacher.

32. Accept reasonable answers. Examples: Beware of people who flatter you just to get what they want.

33. Answers will vary but should recast the fable in shorter sentences, using simpler vocabulary.

34. Answers will vary but may include the following: Use gestures for eating, draw a picture of food or of someone eating, use a translation dictionary to help you say or write a few words, ask (in English) if a classmate speaks English, find a teacher of English and ask her or him.

35. Stories will vary but should include a word from each category.

36. Story beginnings will vary, but the "grabber" should include more interesting language, characters, or events.

Math

37. The table requires the following corrections:
$1 \times 1 = 1$
$4 \times 5 = 20$
$4 \times 7 = 28$
$6 \times 3 = 18$
$7 \times 6 = 42$

38. Answers will vary. The original recipe should total about seven cups, one cup for each hiker, but the total is not as important as using fractions and

making sure the doubled recipe math is correct.
Sample answers:

Trail Mix Recipe:	Doubled Trail Mix Recipe
$1\frac{3}{4}$ cups peanuts	$3\frac{1}{2}$ cups peanuts
1 cup almonds	2 cups almonds
$3\frac{1}{3}$ cups raisins	$6\frac{2}{3}$ cups raisins
$\frac{2}{3}$ cup chocolate chips	$1\frac{1}{3}$ cups chocolate chips

39. Accept all reasonable answers. Students' explanations should reflect an understanding that our number system uses base 10 and that there are repeating patterns in counting from 1 to 100.

40. Sixteenths. Explanations will vary but should include the concept that when a square is divided into sixty-fourths there are more parts, creating a busier effect.

41. (Answers for a ten-year-old)
On Venus:
$10 \times 365 = 3{,}650$, $3{,}650 \div 225 = 16.222$ years old
On Uranus:
$10 \div 84 = .119$ years old

42. Answers will vary.

43. 32,000
Steps will vary. Example: Students might set up a simple algebraic sentence to figure out what the original number was.
1. $x \div 40 = 20$
2. $40 \times 20 = x$
3. $x = 800$
4. $800 \times 40 = 32{,}000$

44. Tom needs to know the distance from the floor to the ceiling (or the height of the sides from ground to where the roof begins).
Or
Tom needs to know the ratio of the height of the shed walls to the length of the sides, the length of the front, or the height from floor to roof peak.

45. Items 1, 3, 4, and 5 are analogies. Items 2 and 6 are not. Item 2 is not an analogy because the order of digits in the first pair is reversed; the second is not. Item 6 is not an analogy because the first relationship can be written 1 : 11; the second cannot.

Daily Warm-Ups: Critical Thinking I

46. 1. Nick 2. Jorge 3. Elliot; Accept accurate explanations. Example: Think of the numbers as compound fractions. 6 feet 7 inches = $6\frac{7}{12}$ feet, 6.7 feet = $6\frac{7}{10}$ feet, 6.07 feet = $6\frac{7}{100}$ feet. $\frac{7}{100}$ is less than $\frac{7}{12}$, which is less than $\frac{7}{10}$.

47. 27 scarves, 18 hats; Students should draw and label a chart showing total items, number of scarves, and number of hats. A good choice would be to show the totals increasing the items by five each time. If students choose that increase, they will note a pattern of increase by three for scarves and by two for hats. Patterns will vary with student choices, but a constant will be the three-to-two ratio of scarves to hats.

48. Accept all reasonable answers.

49. Accept all reasonable questions.

50. Answers will vary. Possible answers: No one would know when to go to work or school. People would not know their birthdays. Stores would have a hard time making any money.

51. Accept all reasonable answers.

52. Milly is incorrect. Her mistake was that in multiplying 450 hundredths by 450 hundredths, she neglected to multiply the denominators as well as the numerators. She also could have avoided her mistake by determining that the two equations are in fact the same. 450 hundredths = 4.50

53. Answers will vary but may include using small objects to show the operations.

54. Diagrams showing the consecutive bounces should prove the statement false. The ball bounces up 3.125 feet on the fifth bounce.

55. Poems will vary.

56. The agreement should include dates and dollar figures. Some students may want to include interest percentages as well.

57. $1 + 3 + 5 + 7 = 16$
$1 + 3 + 5 + 7 + 9 = 25$
Patterns are the odd number sequence 1, 3, 5, 7, and so forth, and the perfect squares sequence 4, 9, 16, 25, and so forth.

Daily Warm-Ups: Critical Thinking I

58. Answers will vary but should include information on rounding numbers. A possibility is to round 34,000 to 30,000 and 365 to 360. Multiply 36 times 3 (108) and write in the correct number of zeros to the answer (five 0's). The estimate will be 10,800,000. To gain further accuracy, students might suggest multiplying 4,000 by 360, by rounding and then adding the necessary 0's (four) to get 1,440,000. Adding this to the first estimate results in 12,240,000. Checking for the accuracy of the estimate, students would multiply 34,000 by 365 to get the exact answer, 12,410,000. Both estimates are close enough to be reasonable.

59. Tonio should fill the five-cup jar and then pour enough in the three-cup jar to fill it. That will leave two cups in the larger jar that he should then pour into his bucket. He should repeat this process and pour another two cups in the bucket that will give him four cups or one quart.

60. $(4 \times 2)1 + 3 - 0 = 11$

61. Oldest to youngest: Keisha, Beth, Steve, Tim; Tallest to shortest: Beth, Keisha, Tim, Steve

62. Answers will vary. Example: Mr. Clayton could make a table listing each student and the price paid for the individual plan. By adding these figures, he can decide that if there are more than five students ($480), he should choose the group rate.

63. Students should draw and label a number line. The first time mail, groceries, and bookmobile arrive on the same day is the 24th day. Another method would be to find the least common multiple of the three numbers 4, 6, and 8.

64. Accept all accurate answers.

65. Students should construct a bar or line graph, showing date on one axis, amount on the other; 3.762 inches

66. Answers will vary but should include enough information to be solvable.

67. Accept reasonable answers. Examples: 1. Weigh 100 beans. Weigh the whole jar. Weigh a similar

Daily Warm-Ups: Critical Thinking I

jar, and subtract that weight. Divide the weight of 100 into the adjusted weight of the whole jar. Multiply this answer by 100. 2. Using graph paper with large squares, count the number of beans that fill one square and then pour out the whole jar on the paper. Count how many squares are covered. Multiply the number of beans in one square by the number of squares.

68. Students should disagree. There are 6 faces, not 5, and there are 12 edges, not 16. Surface area is found by adding the areas of 6 faces. Surface area = 6(4 × 4) = 96 square inches.

69. Accept all reasonable explanations and examples.

70. List should include all measurements of walls, windows, and doorway; cost of paint per gallon; and quantity of paint needed per square foot.

71. Students should draw and label a three-part Venn diagram.

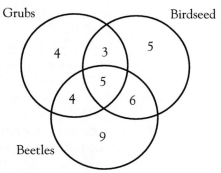

16 eat grubs, 19 eat birdseed, 24 eat beetles

72. Explanations will vary and may include a diagram or verbal explanations that mention the simplifying of fractions to a common denominator.

Social Studies

73. Executive: commander in chief, White House, president, vice president, departments, cabinet, committee, Environmental Protection Agency; Legislative: Congress, senator, representative, amendment, bill, House, district; Judicial:

Supreme Court, judge, judicial, prosecutor, attorney general, appeal, defense

74. Answers will vary but should include the idea that money is representative of value and is exchanged for goods and services.

75. Answers will vary but should convey the understanding that a holiday is a day for people to commemorate an important event or ideal.

76. The best answers will include a description of oceans and an explanation of the water cycle, which causes rain and snow.

77. Answers will vary but should include the concept of participatory government.

78. Messages will vary.

79. Accept all reasonable answers.

80. The following is a complete list of all 50 state names: Alabama, Alaska, Arizona, Arkansas, California, Colorado, Connecticut, Delaware, Florida, Georgia, Hawaii, Idaho, Illinois, Indiana, Iowa, Kansas, Kentucky, Louisiana, Maine, Maryland, Massachusetts, Michigan, Minnesota, Mississippi, Missouri, Montana, Nebraska, Nevada, New Hampshire, New Jersey, New Mexico, New York, North Carolina, North Dakota, Ohio, Oklahoma, Oregon, Pennsylvania, Rhode Island, South Carolina, South Dakota, Tennessee, Texas, Utah, Vermont, Virginia, West Virginia, Washington, Wisconsin, Wyoming

81. Answers will vary. Some students may say that the city will be built in a protected harbor and will use ocean trade. Perhaps mountains provide ore for export, or perhaps the people will fish for a living.

82. Maps will vary but should include symbols, legend, and compass rose.

83. Maps will vary but should include symbols and a map key.

84. Accept reasonable answers, including the following: The store selling the wood wants to make more profit; there is a sudden surge in

house-building, so it is hard to obtain wood; a horrible storm ravaged the forests that produce most of the pine trees; the number of pine trees and amount of pine lumber is naturally dwindling; the cost of fuel for transporting the lumber took a big increase; a rich country bought up most of the supplies of pine recently.

85. Rules will vary but might include the following: obeying the laws, voting, participating in government, being a good neighbor, volunteering in one's community, staying informed, and so on.

86. Answers will vary.

87. Answers will vary.

88. Answers will vary but should defend the form of government students name. For example, in a home democracy there might be family meetings where everyone gets to vote on things, such as where to go for vacation. In a benign dictatorship, one or more parents would make decisions for the good of all.

89. Answers will vary but might include the following: The government represents the people's roots and values; it is wrong to rebel against the government; it is better to settle differences peacefully; the strong British government could defend them in times of trouble; there was no government in place in the new land when the settlers arrived; there was no American system of money or military.

90. Answers will vary.

91. The Statue of Liberty, given to the United States by France in 1886, has come to represent freedom and the sanctuary that this country has provided for immigrants, and therefore, freedom from the tyranny of governments and of poverty. It stands for the liberty offered by the American system of democracy and way of life.

92. Diary entries will vary.

93. Answers will vary but should include the urgent advice not to go to the Ford Theater on the night Lincoln was assassinated.

94. Answers will vary.
95. f. papermaking (100), k. windmills (650), b. eyeglasses (1285), e. modern printing press (1450), h. pencil (1565), j. telescope (1609), i. steam engine (1712), g. parachute (1797), c. lawn mower (1830), d. machine gun (1862), a. bicycle (1867)
96. j. wheelbarrow (230), e. gunpowder (1150), f. mechanical clock (1360), a. artificial limbs (1540), g. pressure cooker (1679), i. submarine (1776), h. sewing machine (1846), b. aspirin (1899), c. ballpoint pen (1938), d. compact disc (1985)
97. Answers will vary but might include parents, friends, siblings, teachers, police officers, librarians, bus drivers, and so on.
98. Answers will vary but may include information about the state's history, climate, landforms, culture, products, people, geography, economy, and so on.

99. Questions will vary but might include the following: When did it occur? Why did people want to trade in slaves? Who were the slaves? Where did they come from? How did people become slaves? What happened to end the slave trade? What happened to slaves when slavery was abolished?
100. Answers will vary.
101. Students should weigh the excitement and other benefits of such a journey against the risks. Reasons will vary.
102. Answers will vary. The book of speeches probably would provide her views on the issue of slavery and perhaps other important issues of the day. However, her personal letters might give a more intimate view of her thoughts and feelings.
103. Answers will vary.
104. Surnames will vary but might include Smith, Sawyer, Piper, Baker, Farmer, Mason, Barber, Singer, Taylor, Tinker, Brewer, Shepherd, Carpenter, Carter, and so on.

Daily Warm-Ups: Critical Thinking I

105. 9 A.M.: Los Angeles; 11 A.M.: Mexico City; 12 noon: Panama City; 5 P.M.: London; 12 midnight: Bangkok; 4 A.M. (the next day): Sydney
106. Answers will vary but may include the following: what the weather is like, how to greet people, what is customary behavior for travelers, what items are not readily available so that she can pack them, and so on.
107. Answers will vary.
108. Answers will vary.

Science

109. 1. Using their senses, students might determine the following: Sight: maximum size of the object, based on width, height, and depth of box. Hearing: Sound coming from box; sound object makes when box is shaken; sound object makes when box is tipped or flipped. Smell: any distinctive smells that are strong enough to be detected through the box material. Touch: The weight of the object. Is the weight evenly distributed? Does the object roll smoothly, roll unevenly, slide, or tumble? Taste: Taste involves contact; this sense does not help. 2. Tools: A magnet might be used to test object for kind of matter. A stethoscope might pick up sounds through the box more clearly. A tape measure or ruler would measure dimensions more precisely. A scale could measure weight more precisely. An X-ray machine could pick up the shape of certain materials.
110. 1. Willow ptarmigans must live someplace where it is an advantage to be white part of the year and brown or mottled at another time. Most likely that means they live anywhere the climate is cold enough to produce snow at certain times of the year. (Ptarmigans live in the northern United States and Canada, where they are white in the winter months and brown in the summer months.) 2. In the spring and fall, they are mottled brown and white. 3. They produce this color change by molting their feathers. 4. This change helps

camouflage them in their environment, which protects them from predators.

111. Answers will vary and may open interesting discussions. (Is the moon a source of light? When it is full, it certainly lights up Earth at night. Is a mirror a source of light?) Any answer backed up by evidence (observation and/or research) is acceptable. Some possible answers: Heat: animals' bodies, microwave oven, rubbing two things together; Heat and Light: sun, magma, light bulb, match, fire, electric stove, candle, toaster, welding torch, lightning; Light: fireflies, phosphorescence

112. Answers will vary but might include erosion marks on rocks; splash marks in sand or dust; pebbles, sand, or other eroded materials deposited in deltas, beaches, dunes, sandbars; sedimentary rocks; some crystallization; cracks in rocks or broken rocks due to ice freezing in cracks; river shapes carved into the land—oxbows, canals, canyons; V-shaped valleys; and U-shaped valleys.

113. Answers will vary but may include the following: The weather influences the choice of clothes and outerwear, some people may have seasonal allergies, the season and growing conditions affect what food is available, weather can affect what sports can be played outside.

114. What could Dr. Bunsen be keeping this powerful substance in? Would it not dissolve the container (and the lab and Earth) as well? If a scientist believes something to be true, it is too easy to design experiments or perform them without adequate controls in order to prove that scientist is correct. Scientists must question observations, test and retest data gathered in controlled experiments, and interpret and critique procedures and data in order to observe accurately and as objectively as possible.

115. 1. whisper, conversation, playground, rock hammer drill 2. tuba, thunder, laugh, scream, piccolo

116. Answers will vary.

Daily Warm-Ups: Critical Thinking I

117. Answers will vary. Some possibilities:
Producers: trees, flowers, grasses
Consumers: deer, grouse, rabbits, squirrels, chickadees, raccoons, porcupines, people, dogs, guinea pigs, spiders
Decomposers: fungi, bacteria

118. Answers will vary. Some possibilities:
Slow changes: weathering, erosion, deposition, plate tectonics, glacial action
Rapid changes: volcanic eruptions, earthquakes, tsunamis, avalanches, comets or meteorites striking Earth, as well as many effects of humans

119. There could be many answers. The most likely is that Dr. Bunsen lives on one side of a mountain range and Professor Quantum lives on the other side. Clouds blowing in from Dr. Bunsen's side of the mountains are forced up, the water vapor cools and condenses, and falls as snow. By the time the clouds are up and over the mountain range, most of the water vapor has condensed and fallen on Dr. Bunsen's side. Professor Quantum, on the lee of the mountain range, is in a kind of precipitation shadow.

120. Answers will vary. Some possibilities:
language arts: understanding of speech production and hearing, development of the computer for word processing, the invention of the printing press, the invention of paper, medical understanding of how people learn to read; math: the invention of the computer for computation, medical understanding of how the brain solves problems, using computer models to show mathematical solutions to problems; social studies: applying the scientific method to sociological studies and surveys, the invention of different modes of travel and communication, medical advances in treating diseases, using the computer to communicate with distant places; physical education: advances in nutrition, medical understanding of mechanical, electrical, and chemical processes of the body,

advances in imaging and measuring for timed competitions; art: using the computer to create art, using chemistry to create paint and other media, using telecommunications to share art and techniques, advances in preservation of ancient art; music: using the computer to generate music, advances in recording technology, using the computer to share music; foreign language: quicker travel, computer translation devices, telecommunications

121. Answers will vary. Some possibilities: lever and fulcrum—seesaw; inclined plane—slide; wheel and axle—merry-go-round, bicycle, skateboard; pulley—possibly on a flag pole; screw—holding equipment together

122. Answers may vary. Hard-boiled eggs spin differently than raw eggs. Because raw eggs have liquid inside the shells, they have more inertia—it is harder for them to start or stop moving. Professor Quantum spun an egg, then stopped it briefly by touching it lightly. An egg with more inertia (a raw egg) would start spinning again when she lifted her finger because the liquid inside it was still moving. An egg with less inertia (a hard-boiled egg) would not start moving again.

123. Answers will vary. Examples of closely interacting systems are the digestive and excretory systems, the circulatory and respiratory systems, or the skeletal and muscular systems.

124. For a garden to produce well, plants need the correct amount of sun, water, and nutrients. They need to withstand pests and disease, competition from weeds, and the ravages of weather extremes. A garden might not produce well if the soil cannot hold water or holds too much; if the soil contains few nutrients or has properties that keep the plant from absorbing nutrients; if trees or buildings block sunlight; if there is little water available (in next-door gardens, this has less to do with rain and more to do with irrigation); if plants are weak

because they were exposed to harsh weather too early or because they should be grown in an area with a different climate; if pests attack weakened plants; if weeds compete for sunlight, water, or nutrients.

125. Students should create a graph showing all the relevant information. Possible explanations should relate to seasonal changes in the northern latitudes, either length of daylight or temperature (heat in August; cold in fall and winter months).

126. Answers will vary. Some possibilities: How are we going to study these communities, since we cannot survive down there, and deep-sea vent organisms cannot survive where we work? Are there any plants? If there is no sunlight, how would plants produce energy? How do the producers in this community produce energy? What are the consumers and decomposers? How do the organisms get oxygen? (At such high pressure, any lung or air bubble would be squashed flat!) How do the organisms deal with the acidity? How do the organisms survive with toxic chemicals such as hydrogen sulfide and heavy metals? How do the organisms cope with temperature changes? Are the organisms similar at different deep-sea vents? What happens to the organisms when a deep-sea vent shuts down? Do they die? Do they find another deep-sea vent? How?

127. A good cough drop might ease a cough, soothe a sore throat, last a long time, taste really good, and cause no unpleasant side effects. To set up an experiment, you would need a number of people with coughs. Before giving out any cough drops, you would record how many times each person coughed in a given amount of time. Then you would divide the test subjects into four groups. Each test subject in a group would be given one kind of cough drop. (They should not be told which kind it is. Ideally, the researcher would not know either. That way no bias would enter the

test.) The fourth group would get candy that looked and tasted like a cough drop. As soon as everyone was sucking on the cough drop, you would observe the times each test subject coughed. You would probably need help observing and recording and might want to include the number of throat clearings as well. To see how long the effects of the cough drops lasted, you would want to continue counting coughs even after the drop had dissolved. Because different people might react differently at different times, you would want to repeat this test at least three times, having each group use a different cough drop each time. To ensure accuracy, you or another person should repeat the entire process two more times.

128. You need milk, though it does not have to be goat's milk. You need something that coagulates or curdles the milk. In the story, it is the inside lining of the goat's stomach, a substance we now call rennet, although there are other substances that do the same thing. The milk needs to be kept at a warm temperature, and at some point, the curd needs to be agitated or stirred. The milk, the coagulating agent, the time, the temperature, the way the curd is cut and stirred, and the way it is pressed at the end are variables that determine the kind of cheese that is made.

129. Answers will vary but should include good nutrition, exercise, rest and sleep, care around germs, dealing with sickness or injury, and avoidance of dangerous substances, such as alcohol, tobacco, and drugs, as well as extremes (weather, exercise).

130. Very carefully, without damaging the plant or the stalk, you can mark certain points on the stalk with thread, ink, or tape. You could place these points near the base, near the buds at the top, or equally spaced all along the stalk. Then every day you could measure and record the distance between the base of the stalk and each of the points, thereby determining the rate of growth of each part of the stalk.

131. The line between instinct and learning is blurry. Scientists disagree, and new discoveries are always being made. Some people believe our brains are built to learn some language, so speaking is instinctual, but speaking a foreign language, such as Swahili, is learned. Some scientists determine instinctual behavior by how universal it is. People all over the world, in many different cultures, blink. They also all learn to speak. Specific languages are different in different cultures, and so are learned. Instinct: smiling, crying, singing, speaking, feeling angry, running, eating, blinking; Learned: playing the guitar, writing poems, cooking spaghetti, brushing teeth, pole-vaulting, speaking Swahili, riding a bike, counting

132. Renewable: trees, soil, freshwater; Nonrenewable: gas, oil, certain kinds of minerals; Inexhaustible: sunlight, water, wind

133. Accept reasonable hypotheses. Some possibilities: The contours of continents in many places seem as if they would be able to fit together like jigsaw puzzle pieces. Types of rocks on the edge of one continent sometimes match rocks on another continent now separated by ocean. Even glacial marks on the rocks sometimes match. Fossils found in South America are very similar to fossils found in Africa. Fossils of tropical organisms have been found in Antarctica, indicating it could have been closer to the equator at one time. Volcanoes, deep-sea vents, and earthquake fault lines indicate edges of plates that make up Earth's surface. Mountain ranges have been pushed up in areas where plates could have collided.

134. Pictures will vary, but examples could be a sunny kitchen scene (radiation) with a pot of noodles cooking on the stove (convection) with a metal spoon sticking out of the pot (conduction).

135. Inventions will vary, but the design must solve a problem and have been evaluated critically.

136. This is a question that many of today's climatologists (and politicians) have a hard time answering. People can have a hard time separating what they think is true from theories based on objective data. Weather systems and climate are so complex, no models can accurately predict next week's weather, let alone next century's climate. When examining competing claims, it is important to look for accurate observations, carefully gathered data, models that reflect observations and data, repetition of experiments by other scientists, and evaluation of experiment procedures by others as well as opportunities to meet, question, and critique scientists with competing theories.

137. Everyone would be relieved for awhile. Even birds and mammals can be bothered by insects. But insects are a vital part of the web of life. They are sources of food for other animals (and even a few plants). They help fertilize flowers. They help break down waste products and dead organisms into nutrients that can be used again.

138. Answers will vary. Questions that are too broad, that are based on opinion, or that are about art or faith cannot be answered by using the scientific process.

139. Since Dr. Skeptic set up the conditions for the test and Aqua Phind agreed to them, she should not get the money because she failed the test. Dr. Skeptic set up a scientific test. Aqua's testimonials, even from sixty people, fail to meet Dr. Skeptic's rules for the test.

140. They are active at different times of the day. Bats fly and feed at night. Swallows feed primarily during dawn and dust. Dragonflies feed primarily in the heat of the day.

141. A physical change may make matter look different, but it remains the same kind of matter. A chemical change causes one kind of matter to become a different kind of matter. In the no-bake cookies, the matter gets mushed up together, but each ingredient remains the same. In the baked

Daily Warm-Ups: Critical Thinking I

cookies, the matter undergoes a change. The soda and eggs react with the other ingredients and the heat of the oven, and the cookies that come out of the oven are different from the ones that went in.

142.   1. mixture: A mixture is a combination of two or more kinds of matter in which the matter can be easily separated: salad, pickles in brine; 2. solution: A solution is a mixture in which two or more kinds of matter are evenly mixed or dissolved together: the brine the pickles are in; 3. solid: Matter is in a solid state if it has definite size and shape: the pickles, ice cubes; 4. liquid: Matter is in a liquid state if it has no definite shape, but has a definite volume: the brine, orange juice, milk; 5. gas: Matter is a gas if it has no definite shape or volume: carbon dioxide bubbles in a soda

143.   Answers will vary.

144.   Poems will vary but could include words such as rain, snow, hail, sleet, clouds, cumulus, cirrus, nimbus, thunderhead, thunder, lightning, blizzard, tornado, hurricane, cyclone, low pressure, high pressure, temperature, water cycle, precipitation, condensation, evaporation.

Life Skills

145.   Answers will vary. The best answers will include items with multiple uses, such as rope, matches, and a fold-up saw or other tools. Students should also include food and water supplies.

146.   Students should never enter a car with a stranger, no matter what the circumstances are. Answers might include declining politely, reentering the school, calling parents, or calling the uncle to confirm the safety of the driver.

147.   Rules will vary but might include never opening the door; having emergency numbers at hand; having no visitors; checking in with a neighbor or family friend; and refraining from using the stove.

148.   Advice will vary. The best answer will take into account the possibility that the grandmother could have problems taking care of herself. Perhaps live-in help or a medical exam would be possible solutions.

149. Advice will vary but should make some attempt at conflict resolution.
150. Advice will vary but might include the child airing his feelings, the family agreeing on rules, or a session with a family counselor.
151. Answers will vary.
152. Answers will vary but might include writing down the name or number of the row in which the car is parked; standing at the door of the mall and noting which row and direction to take to find the car; making a little sketch of where the car is; remembering where the car is in relation to something else, such as a light pole or a carriage corral; or making up a mnemonic to help remember where it is.
153. Answers will vary. Some students may say it is safest just to push the bike the rest of the way. If there are places with helpers on the way home, such as a police or a fire station, Ike might stop there. It is safest not to ask for help from strangers.
154. Answers will vary but should avoid harshly judging or berating the friends and focus on "I statements."
155. Answers will vary.
156. The apple is clearly the healthiest snack; however, some students may feel that the crackers and cheese, since they include some protein, would be a better choice, since dinner is three hours away. You may want to point out that sugary snacks provide a quick boost in energy but leave a person feeling hungry again after a short time.
157. Answers will vary. While circumstances have changed and formality has loosened, the basis of good manners remains the same—respect for the feelings of others.
158. Answers will vary but should include reasons for the decision.
159. Answers will vary but should include specific strategies for obtaining money for the bicycle.

160. Budgets will vary but should include a plan for building some savings.

161–164. Answers will vary but should include rationales for each choice.

165. Answers will vary but may include the following. Math: balancing a checkbook, figuring a budget, measuring, figuring area of a floor or yard, computing cost per unit at the supermarket, figuring interest, computing taxes; Language Arts: writing letters, creating a resume, giving a speech or a toast, using a dictionary, writing a report at work, understanding instructions, reading instructions on a prescription, reading a menu, helping a child with homework; Science: recycling properly, identifying birds or animals, propagating seeds or other gardening tasks, avoiding accidents involving mixing of cleaning substances, understanding doctors, choosing healthy foods, making healthy choices about exercise

166. Students should choose some of the most useful or important words and phrases to know, such as *Excuse me, please, thank you, where is . . ., taxi, airport, hotel, restroom, restaurant, Can you help me?* and *emergency*.

167. Telling is the right thing to do. Al might become addicted to alcohol and hurt himself or others if you do not tell. However, telling does put the friendship at risk.

168. Answers will vary. The student might be able to arrange to take the test again to prove his or her innocence. If the student is guilty, the best course in probably to admit it and ask for a way to make amends.

169. Preferences and rationales will vary. Swimming is good exercise and is an important skill to know for safety reasons. Music is also a lifelong enjoyment for many people, and band can also be a fun social activity.

170. Plans should be realistic and include both sensible eating habits and an exercise schedule.

Answer Key

171. Answers will vary, but items on the list indicate the siblings are going somewhere cold, sunny, and at a high altitude. Perhaps they are going to climb Mount Everest.
172. Answers will vary.
173. The emergency call to 911 should be made first. The student can still grab the fire extinguisher and try to extinguish the blaze as well. If the fire extinguisher is used first, before the emergency call is made, the fire might get out of control before help arrives.
174. Headings in the Yellow Pages: furniture, used furniture, antiques, spinning wheels, consignment shops, furniture reproductions. Other sources: newspaper advertisements, swap pages, the Internet, antique stores, flea markets
175. Accept reasonable answers. Healthy habits include eating fresh fruits and vegetables, exercising, drinking lots of water, getting enough sleep, taking time for leisure and enjoyment, doing yoga, and meditating. Unhealthy habits include eating sugar or too many calories, eating junk food, staying up late, smoking, drinking, taking drugs, and overworking.
176. Solutions will vary but might include having a vacation at home, taking Barkley along, hiring a pet sitter, asking a family member to take the dog, asking a vet if there is medication to help Barkley stay calm, taking the dog to a kennel every day for a month until it is more used to it, and finding someone who cares for dogs in a home environment.
177. Answers will vary.
178. Answers will vary but should reflect self-appraisal.
179. Answers will vary but may include calling a pest control company, putting a branch or board into the pool as a ramp, luring the animal out with food, using a crane to pluck out the animal, using another skunk to lure the animal.

Daily Warm-Ups: Critical Thinking I

180.   Answers will vary. Some possibilities: Every child should get to go to Disney World. I will be so disappointed if we cannot go. What can I do to convince you to go? I will clean my room and take out the trash for a year if you take me. Crime is almost nonexistent there. Once we arrive, you will not have to drive at all. It is very educational. I will pay for my own ticket.